OpenSource

Astrophotography

*Your first low cost astro photo
from your backyard*

For my wife Dagmar, who had to give up a lot of our spare time for this book.

Contents

Table of Contents

Preface

Astrophotography is a great hobby, but it is generally considered to be difficult, expensive and time consuming. In this book I describe my way of overcoming these problems.

The benefit of open source software is not only the reduction of the financial burden. It also facilitates the implementation of the hobby by a variety of software tools that are easy to install and a useful remedy for the problems in astrophotography. I use UBUNTU Linux and all the examples in this book use the software on this operating system. The software is platform independent (except fotoxx) and runs as well on Windows or Mac.

The focus of the hardware, which is described in this book, is also located in the low-cost area. A digital SLR or a mirrorless system camera is sufficient to start with. Important are ports for connecting interchangeable lenses, especially for a T2 adapter. No further adaptation is needed. The camera is mounted on the focuser of the telescope using the T2 adapter. In case you don't have a system camera with interchangeable lenses, a normal digital camera will do. In this case you might want to use a "digital mount", which holds the camera in front of the eyepiece.

Which telescope you want to use depends on your wallet. For getting started in astrophotography, you can safely use an inexpensive achromatic refractor telescope. If necessary this can be later used as a guide scope.

The telescope with a camera must finally be fixed on on a tripod or better on an equatorial mount. At this point, it becomes expensive: Even beginners should prefer a stable equatorial mount to a cheap "wobble mount". If you give up the hobby, a GOTO mount is easily sold on eBay.

After this introduction, I hope you will enjoy reading the book, have a lot of success with the implementation of the content and a lot of satisfaction when looking at the results.

One note to my language skills: This book is the translation of my German language book "OpenSource Astrophotografie 2.0". I apologize for any translation errors.

Karl Sarnow
December 2012

Principles of
Astrophotography

Spaceship earth is your location

First of all: The earth is the spaceship in which we move through space and shoot images of our astronomical companions. This has consequences: Unlike in photography, astrophotographers have no firm stand on which to mount the camera, because the earth rotates once every 24 hours around its polar axis. And any mount on earth follows with the same speed. The movement is visible with the naked eye. We might want to capture the movement perhaps as star trails later on in an aesthetically pleasing image.

But as you know, through a telescope every movement seems faster. That is why telescopes at tourist viewpoints are on tripods. Looking through such a sturdy tripod at the night sky, you can see the stars move at a constant speed through the field of view.

In order to take pictures of the night sky with a telescope, we have to move the telescope at the rotational velocity of the earth in the opposite direction. With this we make up for the rotation of the earth and the starry sky appears to be at a standstill in the telescope. Now we can also use long exposure times to shoot pictures of the stars. We therefore want to use a telescope that controls this reverse rotation with the help of a motor (figure 1).

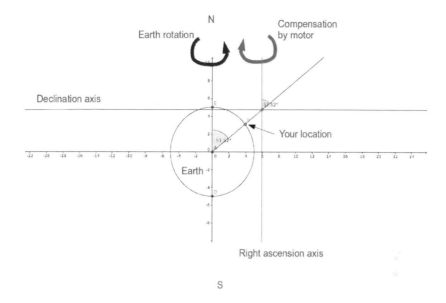

Figure 1: Compensation of earth rotation by motor in an equatorial telescope mount.

You will recognize, that the earth's rotation is compensated by a rotation around an axis parallel to the North-South axis. This parallel to the north-south axis in the telescope mount is called the right ascension axis (also called polar axis). If the motor is turned on, it follows the visible star in the telescope. The angle in the center of the earth is the latitude. It is 0° on the equator and +90 ° at the north pole. At the south pole the latitude is -90°. When properly aligned, the right ascension axis must show the same angle at the mount as the local latitude. Figure 2 shows a simple equatorial mount.

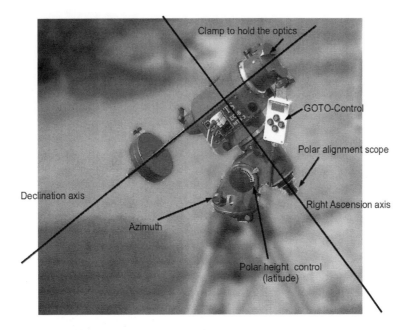

Figure 2: An equatorial telescope mount.

To set up the mount, it is rotated on the tripod in the azimuth right-left, until the polar alignment scope points toward Polaris (figure 3). Then move the mount up-down using the polar height control until Polaris is in the marking of the polar alignment scope.

To select any star, the telescope must be rotated around a second axis. This axis is perpendicular to the right ascension and is called the declination axis (figure 2). The rotation angle of right ascension and declination defines the location of an astronomical object (star, galaxy, ...). They are its coordinates. Unfortunately, however, the mount rotates continuously around the right ascension axis. Therefore, it was agreed that the the right ascension angle starts a certain point in the sky, the vernal equinox. Once the telescope is concentrated at this point, the angle of right ascension is 0h. It is actually measured in hours and not as usual in degrees.

Sky coordinates

The star Alcor, for example, the Little Horseman above the Big Dipper has the coordinates RA = 13h25m22s and DEC = 54 ° 55m28s. How can we find the star with an equatorial mount?

- Set up the mount and align the right ascension axis parallel to the earth.
- Align the telescope to the vernal equinox.
- Turn to the right ascension to 13h25m22s.
- Turn the declination for 54° 55m28s.

The star is now visible in the eyepiece of the telescope. Quite simple, isn't it? There still remain some simple questions.

- How will I know that the right ascension axis is aligned parallel to the axis of the earth?
- How do I find the vernal equinox?
- How can the right ascension be set to 13h25m22s, while the right ascension axis is constantly rotating?

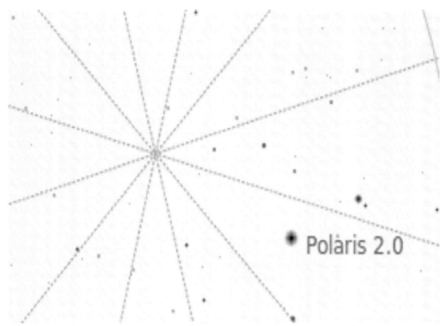

Figure 3: Polaris is near the celestial north pole.

For the alignment of the right ascension axis (first question), there is a simple tool, the polar alignment finder. The mount is first aligned roughly to the north. You will find the letter **N** somewhere on the mount to help with rough alignment. Through the hollow right ascension axis, a small telescope with a marker, the polar alignment scope, looks into the sky. Coincidentally, there is a star located close to the celestial north pole, called Polaris (figure 3). The telescope is now aligned by rotating the azimuth (right-left) and the latitude (up-down) so that Polaris shows in the marking of the polar alignment scope (figure 4). As this procedure is quite easy, make sure your mount has a polar alignment scope built in.

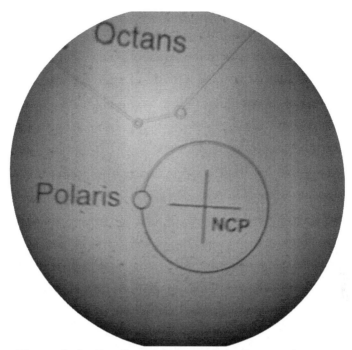

Figure 4: A view through the polar alignment scope.

The second and third questions cannot be answered that simply. The easiest way is to engage the computer. However, in order to help the computer must be built in the mount and control the declination and right ascension axis. This is the case when the mount is advertised as equatorial GOTO-mount. If reading the right ascension is a problem for you, the equatorial GOTO-mount is the solution. Once you have aligned the mount using the polar alignment scope as described, switch on the computer in the mount. The computer asks for a known visible star. After verification, you move the mount with the arrow keys on the remote control panel to the specified star and confirm on the control panel. That's it. Now you only need to enter the desired object. The telescope moves thanks to the GOTO control to the desired object, which should then be visible in the middle of the eyepiece. More or less. Again, locating an object using the right ascension is a problem for you, you should insist on a GOTO mount. In this book, I assume that you have followed my advice and I will limit myself to the description of the use of a GOTO mount, if that should be necessary at all.

The super-stable tripod

A properly aligned equatorial mount is now actually something like the tripod for astrophotographers. With careful alignment, exposure times of up to one minute without tracking control are possible. But good astrophotography occasionally requires exposure times of hours. So what to do then? In this case helps a second telescope, the guide scope, which is mounted parallel to the photographing scope. A digital camera at the back of the guide scope monitors a star continuously. Whenever the star moves in the guide scope, the digital camera sends a signal to the equatorial mount and brings it back on track. This procedure is called autoguiding and makes a GOTO mount a super stable mount, which allows exposure times of almost any length.

Proposals for the beginner

There are equatorial GOTO mounts available in the price range from € 500 to € 10,000. My experience is based on the HEQ5 and EQ6 mounts from Skywatcher, a low-cost Chinese manufacturer. Alternatively, the Celestron CAMGoto, Skywatcher EQ3Skyscan or Orion SkyView Pro Equatorial GoTo Telescope Mount, just to name 3 models, are examples of other inexpensive equatorial GOTO mounts. They all have a clamp for the GP scope base. Most tele-scopes come with such a dovetail plate and can be mounted directly to the clamp. For astrophotography avoid GOTO mounts that are not equatorial mounts. Most of these are less suitable for photogra-phy and use a fork mount or one arm mount. Check with your re-tailer. For visual observations however these mounts are un-matched practical and handy.

The equipment needed

The mount

The mount is that part of the telescope, which carries the optics. It guarantees a centered object throughout the exposure time. Additionally, the mount (or better the built in computer) should allow fast finding of objects. And last but not least, the mount must be stable enough to carry the weight of the optics with the attached camera and be so sturdy not start swinging in the wind. Below the mount is a tripod or column, holding contact to the earth. Normally both the mount and the tripod are sold as a set. As mentioned in the chapter *Principles of astrophotography* you should own or buy an equatorial GOTO mount.

The optics

The actual telescope optics consist of either a lens telescope (refractor) or a mirror telescope (reflector). If you want to start this hobby from scratch, a combination of equatorial GOTO mount and optics is a good idea. If necessary, you can later exchange the optics. For starters, it should be a design with not too long a focal length. A large aperture would be good because it allows short exposure times but it is also expensive. For the beginner, the following chart may be helpful (table 1).

Type	Advantage	Disadvantage	Price range	Remark
Achromatic lens (Refractor, lens telescope)	Low cost.	chromatic aberration, low aperture.	€ 200-500	Low cost lens telescope. Less recommended for ambitious amateurs. Well usable for hobby starters.
Apochromatic lens (Refractor, lens scope)	Good imaging quality. Large aperture.	Expensive, Heavy.	€ 400-5000	Recommendable for ambitious amateurs. Focus length below 1000mm. Best for wide field photos.
Newton scope (Reflector, mirror scope)	Good imaging quality. Large aperture. Low cost.	Heavy, high level of maintenance.	€ 100-5000	Recommendable for ambitious amateurs. All focal lengths and apertures available. Requires more sturdy mounts due to the size of the scope. The mirrors must be adjusted frequently. Less for beginners.
Maksutov-Cassegrain scope (Mirror scope with lenses)	Good image quality. Low cost. Long focal length. Reduced maintenance efforts.	Small aperture, long focal length.	€ 300-1000	Small aperture and long focal length require long exposure times. Therefore a better mount is recommended. For more experienced amateurs.
Schmidt-Cassegrain scope (Mirror scope with lenses)	Good imaging quality. Long focal length. Low maintenance efforts.	Small aperture, long focal length.	€ 500-7000	Like Maksutov-Cassegrain. Very good image quality, more for the ambitious amateur.

Table 1: Overview on scope types.

The beginner telescope for astrophotographers should be easy to transport, so you are ready for quick imaging. Thus a combination of a small GOTO mount with a small refractor is suitable for a first taste. With about € 700 you are ready to go. But if you are not sure if this investment is worth it, a step by step introduction is given in the chapter "The first observation night".

The camera

The most important criterion of a camera for astrophotography is its sensitivity to light. However, we are not talking about special cameras for astrophotography since those can easily reach the price range of € 10,000. No, let's go with a simple digital camera that we already own. If you think astrophotography is fun, you can still purchase a special astro camera.

Once you look at the digital camera market, you can distinguish between the following types of digital cameras:

- Digital SLR. This type has an optical viewfinder through the lens. Maybe this seems a bit outdated, but it is not. No other viewfinder will allow you to see things in darkness like an optical viewfinder. Unique features are the interchangeable lenses that are mounted to the camera by a bayonet. Newer members of this category have a "live view" setting. If this feature is turned on, the mirror pops up and opens the optical pathway to the image sensor. The image can then be observed directly on the camera screen. This option is best suited to adjust the focus of the telescope.
- Digital system camera. This is on one hand the advanced development of the digital SLR camera without a mirror, on the other hand a return to the good old Ur-Leica, and other representatives of cameras with interchangeable lens, but without a mirror for the TTL viewfinder. These cameras also have a bayonet mount for interchangeable lenses, yet with-

out the mirror, and only a "Live View" mode viewfinder. For astrophotography this means, that you will not see objects except bright stars. Nevertheless, this is what you need for focusing.

- Digital camera with fixed lens. The traditional digital camera that can be used for afocal photography and Star Trails.

Particularly suitable because of the interchangeable lenses are only the SLR (optimally with Live View mode) and the system cameras. You can start with the normal digital camera, but very quickly feel the desire for a better solution.

In each case, the camera should allow manual adjustment of exposure, sensitivity and, in the case of a digital camera with fixed lens, a manual focus adjustment.

The camera's ISO sensitivity is one of the most important features. Here, however, considerable scepticism is recommended. It is important that the camera at high sensitivity is not too noisy. If you plan to purchase a new camera, read the test reports carefully. They normally do report about the behaviour at higher ISO settings. In my case, I shoot with 6400ISO sensitivity and get quite usable shots (see below). Therefore, I recommend in any case a camera with at least 6400ISO sensitivity to look for. The table below shows a selection of cameras with high maximum sensitivity.

Camera (Selection)	Maximal ISO-Sensitivity	Price (2012 in Europe)
Nikon D4	204800	from € 5700
Canon EOS 6D	102400	from € 2000
Pentax K5	51200	from € 1000
Canon EOS 650D	25600	from € 600

Camera (Selection)	Maximal ISO-Sensitivity	Price (2012 in Europe)
Nikon D5100	25600	from € 450
Olympus E-PL5	25600	from € 700
Sony NEX-5	25600	from € 500
Panasonic LUMIX GH2	12800	from € 800
Samsung NX1000	12800	from € 450

Focal astrophotography

You need a camera with an interchangeable lens. Either a system camera or a digital SLR. If the sensitivity is high enough, you may have such short exposure times that you can take photos of astronomical objects without autoguiding. This simplifies the start with astrophotography. Later you can still upgrade to guided astrophotography. But first you have to have a first success. You will need a T2 adapter for your camera. In the past when the world was taking photos with analog SLR cameras, it was possible to connect all brands of lenses to cameras of nearly all manufacturers of the world. The trick: The lens had a T2 thread. And for each camera, there was a T2 adapter that fitted to the camera. The lens was then screwed onto the T2 adapter and worked fine on each camera for which a T2 adapter existed. And that was virtually any camera on the market. Astrophotographers today adapted that trick. There are eyepiece tubes with a T2 thread that fit into the eyepiece holder of the telescope. At the end of the eyepiece tube, the T2 adapter of the camera takes the digital SLR or system camera. Now the camera and the telescope are a photographic unit. The image sensor of the camera is located in the focal plane of the telescope. (figure 5). This is the technique of professional astrophotographers and we make it ours.

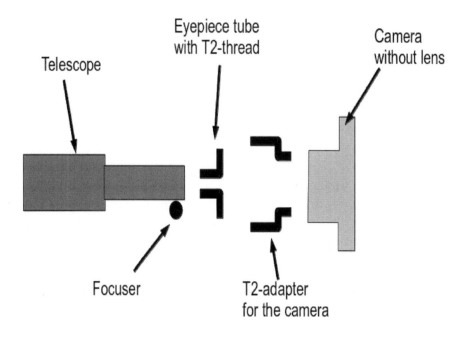

Figure 5: Connecting a camera with interchangeable lens to the telescope with a T2-adapter.

As said in the beginning, we restrict ourselves to amateur astrophotography cameras that are already present in the household of the reader. It should not be a secret that professional astrophotography is done only with special cooled image sensors. But this is a different league. Even DSLR or system cameras might not be available in your household so far. Nevertheless you can start with a standard digital camera, if you are not too ambitious with the selection of your objects.

Afocal astrophotography

For this technique, a classic digital camera of either quality category will suffice. Helpful would be a manual focusing. Set the focus to infinity and attach the prepared camera to the eyepiece with an eyepiece camera mount (figure 6).

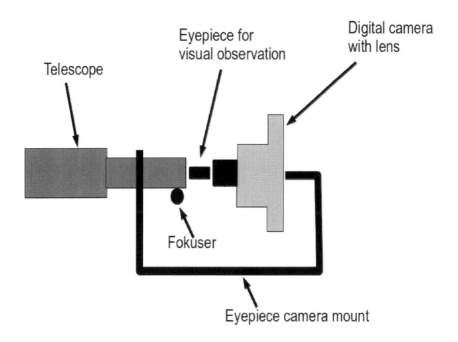

Figure 6: A standard digital camera is fixed to the eyepiece with an eyepiece camera mount.

Focusing is done with the focuser of the telescope, the lens of the camera remains set to infinity.

There are also special photo eyepieces available, where the eyepiece itself has a T2-thread to directly connect to the lens of the camera. If the camera lens has a filter thread, as cameras had in analog times, there are adapter rings available that connect the eyepiece with T2-thread directly to the filter threads of the camera lens.

Unfortunately, modern digital cameras do not have filter threads any more.

Afocal projection

In this variant, a photo eyepiece with T2-thread is used to directly project the image of the astronomical object onto the image sensor of the camera. The advantage is to increase the focal length of the telescope. Unfortunately this also requires a camera with a remov-able lens (figure 7).

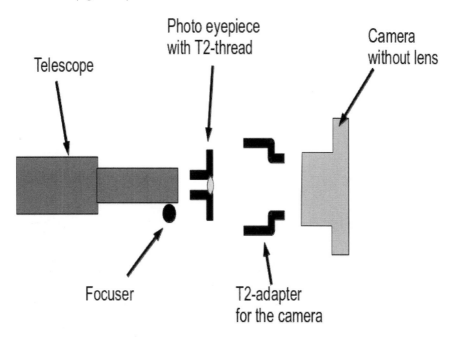

Figure 7: Using afocal projection, the enlarged image on the image sensor is created by the eyepiece.

Astrophotography without a telescope

Of course you can take astrophotos directly with the built in lens. For this purpose, you should consider two arrangements:

- Photography with a photo tripod. The camera is not moved by a motor. The stars are therefore not shown as dots but draw a circular line around Polaris.
- Mounting the camera with lens on the equatorial mount. There are GP-rails with a screw thread for connecting the camera. Then, the camera can be tracked with its own lens. Depending on the quality of the lens and the camera, you can achieve pretty wide field images.

In both cases, the focus of the lens should be set manually to infinity. If your camera does not have a manual focus setting, it will probably fail taking astronomical images using either of these two methods.

The shooting

Depending on the chosen method, the focus is set by the telescope focuser or the built in lens. The focus is controlled either directly on the display of the camera or a digital SLR optical viewfinder. If the digital SLR has a Live View mode, you should use it for focusing, but you will be limited to bright stars. So first align your camera to a bright star and then focus it. Do not change this focus setting while moving to other objects. For re-focusing, you have to move again to a bright star, because live view viewfinders are not able to detect low intensity astronomical objects.

If your camera allows you to manually set the shutter speed, set the longest possible exposure time (before the B setting, B for bulb). Allow up to 30 seconds at the maximum sensitivity of the camera (e.g. 6400ISO) for impressive pictures of the night sky. And always take more than one photo from the same object. I do always take 10 images for later adding of images with the GIMP.

My own technical equipment

Maybe it is interesting for beginners, what equipment I'm currently using to take my photos. Therefore, I have compiled table 2. My equipment is not professional and is based on my tight budget. Moreover, for me the quick setup and portability is important. The equipment is certainly not sufficient to fill a glossy book on astrophotography with superb Hubble quality images. But most of my friends are impressed by the quality achieved. Examples of photos made with this equipment can be found in [2].

Device	Price (ca. 9/2012 in Germany)	Features
Skywatcher HEQ5 Pro Synscan equatorial GOTO mount	€ 944	Very transportable, easy to align, easy to operate equatorial GOTO mount.
ETX90 Maksutov-Cassegrain Telescope f=1250mm, d=90mm	€ 829	Very small, very light, excellent image quality. Built in flip mirror to switch between visual observation and photography. My version is a bit older and has no GOTO part. The mentioned price is with GOTO fork mount. I removed the old (non-GOTO) fork mount and put the telescope tube on a GP dovetail plate. Meanwhile there are similar telescopes from Asian manufacturers for a lesser price, if you do not need the GOTO fork mount.
Orion ED80 achromatic refractor	€ 119	Small achromatic corrected lens scope with acceptable image quality. Originally intended to be

Device	Price (ca. 9/2012 in Germany)	Features
f=400mm, d=80mm		used as a guide scope. But as it has a built in T2-thread, it is also very useful for wide field images.
Astro Professional ED102 Refraktor f=714mm, d=102mm	€ 850	Larger apochromatic corrected lens scope with good image quality.
GSO Newton type mirror scope f=800mm, d=200mm	€ 478	Very bright photographic Newton mirror telescope. Must be adjusted once before every observation night. A 2" coma corrector should be used to protect the image sensor and avoid coma in the photo. Very heavy and therefore less suitable for transportation.
Camera Olympus E-410.	n.a.	This older DSLR camera has a FourThirds mount (FT). It is no longer available. Successors are system cameras with the Micro-FourThirds mount (MFT). The small image sensor size (half of 35mm film size negatives), triggers an effective doubling of the focal length of the telescope. With ISO1600 much less sensitive than my NIKON D5100 DSLR. This camera was one of

Device	Price (ca. 9/2012 in Germany)	Features
		the first ones with Live View mode.
Camera Nikon D5100	€ 500	DSLR-Camera with up to 25600ISO sensitivity. The turn-able monitor in combination with the Live View mode allows sim-ple focusing without turning the neck. All photos I made with this camera were taken with 6400ISO and 30s exposure time at all tele-scopes without guiding.

Table 2: My personal equipment.

Actually it turns out that careful alignment of the mount and taking advantage of the highest sensitivity level of new camera models with the longest exposure time of less than B (30s on the Nikon, Olympus in the 60s), the images from all telescopes show round stars, the criterion for no movement while the shutter was open. If the stars are not round, some shift occurred with open shutter.

OpenSource Software for Astrophotography

There are two species of software useful for astrophotography:
- Software for the preparation of the observation night.
- Software for processing the results of the observation night.

The first type of software helps you to select the objects to be observed and supports the alignment of the mount. The tools are called Kstars [5] and Stellarium [6].

Kstars is a cross-platform software for the display of the night sky in the form of maps. Anywhere in the world at any time. On the Kstars maps you can find 100 million stars, 13.000 deep sky objects, all 8 planets, the sun and moon, and thousands of comets and asteroids.

Stellarium has similar features, but the Stellarium screen shows the sky in a photo realistic way. That is, at daylight you do not see stars but the sun and (sometimes) the moon. At twilight time, some zones of the screen are light, others are already dark and the brightest stars appear. Later on, the sky is shown as as seen from a desert. Nevertheless, in any case dew and atmospheric influence is visible. You can even display the landscape in the area, showing visibility restrictions by surrounding trees and buildings. There is also a manual on how to bring in your actual observation space into the Stellarium night.

The result of a well prepared observation night should be a set of astronomical photos. But these are not as brilliant as those found in glossy books about astronomy. They are in urgent need of refurbishment with a suitable image processing software. GIMP [4] is the tool of choice for this task. And once you are finished with GIMP, you might in some cases consider Fotoxx [16] for the final touch of HDR (High Dynamic Range) or stacked image processing. Unfortunately Fotoxx is so far only available for the LINUX operating system, although it is OpenSource. So maybe the program's source code is just waiting for you to translate it to Windows or Mac machines.

Kstars

At this point, I will describe how Kstars is used to prepare for the observation night. The first step is telling Kstars where you are located. This is done through the menu "*Settings | Geographic*". This opens a menu with local proposals (figure 8). Simply choose a nearby city.

Figure 8: The geographic selection window of Kstars.

The first step to observation is the installation of the telescope. For this purpose, the mount has to be aligned with the polar scope. With this scope you locate Polaris, the north star. Unfortunately Polaris is not located exactly at the sky's north pole (NCP: North Celestial

Pole). Like all stars it rotates around the nearby NCP. Kstars shows you where Polaris is located exactly at the specified time (figure 3). If you rotate the polar finder scope around the right ascension axis as Kstars shows Polaris, the mount is aligned quite accurately. However, it should be noted that the polar finder scope is a simple Kepler type telescope. This means that the view is an image reversed view. So you should arrange the polar finder scope as indicated in figure 9: A thought red line goes through Polaris in Kstars, the NCP in Kstars, the NCP in the polar finder scope and Polaris in the polar finder scope.

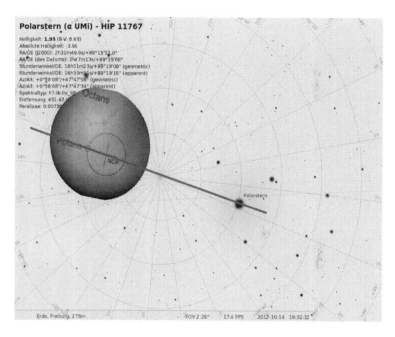

Figure 9: Kstars helps finding the correct alignment of the polar finder scope.

Then bring Polaris into the polar finder scopes marking by adjusting the azimuth angle (right-left) and the altitude angle (up-down).

The next steps in using the equatorial mount is the alignment to the spring equinox. Using a GOTO mount you simply have to select a bright star from a list, which you can clearly identify in the sky. Stellarium is better for this purpose, because the photo-realistic rendering supports the novice in the selection of a brilliant reference star. But Kstars also helps finding a suitable reference star.

To find the most suitable reference star for the calibration, the simple sky view is sufficient. It depends on the direction in which you have a clear view on the observation night (figure 10).

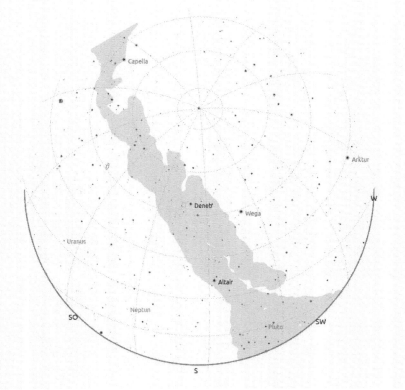

Figure 10: In the sky view you can choose the brightest stars as reference stars for the alignment of the mount (Inverse display).

If bright stars are seen, whose names are not listed, you can activate the context menu with a right click of the mouse and select the "Add label" entry.

In the above case, I would have chosen the Altair as a reference star because it was clearly visible in the southern sky.
Once found, select it in the GOTO control. The telescope turns to the position where it assumes the star. You then have to move the scope using the GOTO control until the selected star is visible in the center of the eyepiece. Calibration done!

Now you can choose any object from the database of the GOTO control unit. Kstars can help you finding an interesting object in the dialog "*Tools | What's Up Tonight*" (figure 11).

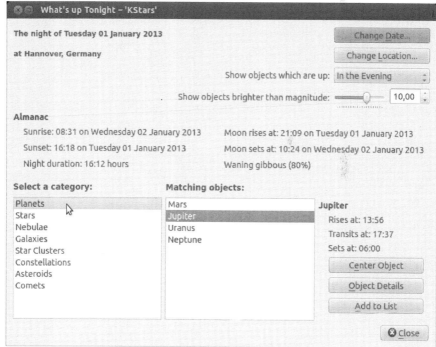

Figure 11: The dialogue presents the visible objects at the selected location.

This will be described in detail in the chapter "*The first observation night*".

Stellarium

Stellarium particularly impresses by its aesthetics. Stellarium therefore is the program more likely to be used. Also in the choice of reference stars, the photo-realistic rendering of the sky is useful.

The selection of the reference star is indeed most impressive. The corresponding sky view figure 12 shows a bright star in the southern sky (Altair). By clicking on it (circle) its data is shown in the upper left corner.

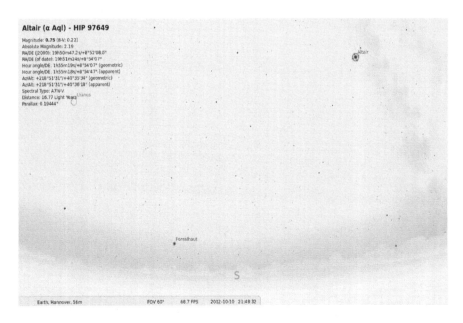

Figure 12: Stellarium shows the photo realistic night sky (Inverted display).

Again, in the section "*The first observation night*" I will explain how to use Stellarium for planning the observation at night.

GIMP

GIMP [4] is used after the results of the observation night are on the hard disk. The following tasks are done with GIMP:

- Most astrophotos are affected with artifacts that need to be removed. The most important task is to compensate the lightning of the night sky in a city.
- The low brightness of astronomical objects requires the summation of many underexposed shots into a good exposed one.
- With long exposure times the image sensors noise increases. This noise is shown in a grainy structure, which can be removed by softening the image and/or averaging many noisy images into one without noise.
- By changing the brightness curve, fine image details can be worked out.

All this I will discuss in detail in the chapter "*After taking photos*".

Fotoxx

Fotoxx [16] is a combination of photographic archive and image editing software. For astronomy use, its capability to handle image clusters like HDR and image stacking is most important. This includes everything that has been listed under GIMP already. Fotoxx can not do anything that GIMP could not do as well. But especially for the creation of HDR (High Dynamic Range) images, Fotoxx is particularly easy to operate. Likewise, the image noise reduction by stacking of 2-9 images is easy. It is very easy to combine images by stacking and painting. Fotoxx starts operation after the images have been treated by GIMP. As I wrote before:

All this I will discuss in detail in the chapter "*After taking photos*".

The first observation night

Here we are: By way of exception a clear sky announces a good observation night early in the evening (Yes, I am living in a rainy part of the world). Now you should plan the objects you would like to observe at night. Helpful can be Kstars "What's up tonight" or a look at the Stellarium sky. Then choose your favorite and get ready.

In the afternoon with Kstars

Date, time and location are set in Kstars using the menu entry "*Time | Set Time*" and "*Settings | Geographic*". Usually you will not take photos from a mountain but from your garden, which is surrounded by trees and buildings. So it's good to know beforehand which items you do not need to look for.

For the beginner, star clusters are the most rewarding objects, followed by galaxies and nebulae. Planets require a large focal length of the telescope. Less than one meter focal length is not promising for photos of planets. Two meter focal length and more provide better images but require a massive and sturdy mount. Therefore, we slowly work our way ahead into the first photo night and focus on globular star clusters. When we see one for the first time in the eyepiece, we understand the name: Like a snowball of thousands of suns it is clear to distinguish from the surrounding stars. Table 3 shows a list of globular star clusters from the Messier list [1].

Object	Brightness [mag]	Viewing angle
M2	6,3	16'
M3	6,2	18'
M5	6,65	23'
M10	6,6	20'
M13	5,8	20'
M15	6,2	18'
M22	5,5	32'
M92	6,3	14'

Table 3: Easy to observe globular star clusters [1].

The brightness in table 3 is measured by a specification, in which a smaller number means a brighter object. The viewing angle gives a measure of the size of the cluster in the eyepiece. Stellarium offers a tool to check the appearance of the object in the eyepiece, which Kstars does not have. The selection of globular clusters in table 3 is restricted to those with a brightness 7 or smaller (brighter) and viewing angles over 10'. Thus, these objects are clearly visible even in small telescopes.

To test whether the object can be seen today in our environment, we are looking for it with the menu item "*Pointing |Find object*" or by clicking on the small binocular icon in the upper left menu bar. Then we choose "globular clusters" for the type filter and/or enter the name of a globular cluster in the name filter. If the object is visible in the sky, then the FOV symbol moves to the corresponding point on the map and you can decide whether the object will be visible or hidden by trees or houses. Otherwise the object might be below the horizon. Then you will see nothing but green ground.

Figure 13: The globular cluster M13 is centered in the map, marked by the red FOV-symbol (Telrad finder). The details window shows astronomical details, including an image.

In figure 13 you can see that I have selected M13 from the list of globular clusters. A right click on the the map opens the context menu:

- A click on "Details" opens the detail window with a photo of the object.
- "Center and track" moves the object in the center of the map and keeps it there while time goes on.
- "Add to observation wish list" does what it says.

In the "*Settings | FOV symbols*" menu you can choose different viewfinder symbols (Here: red circles for Telrad finder) to mark the location of M13. As M13 at this time and location is located far to the west (SW), my telescope would just look into my bedroom. So I better look for another object. M15 would be well visible in the south. So I take M15 into my watch list, while I click "Add to observation wish list".

We repeat the tagging of all the objects that we have planned for that night. To save some work, let's put all objects from table 3 to the watchlist. So before dusk, we have completed the watchlist.

A bit more convenient is the setup wizard. With active observation wish list (Tools | Observing list) click on WUT (What's Up Tonight). Unfortunately, just for globular clusters Kstars 2.0.0 under Ubuntu 12.04 LTS are not accessible due to a bug: All globular clusters are stored without their brightness. As the WUT tool needs the brightness as a selection criterion, it fails just for globular clusters. Fortunately, the "Add object" tool (see figure 13) is nearly as useful as the WUT tool.

Once the selection process is finished, you have the observation wish list ready. Now you can go further setting up the session plan (figure 14).

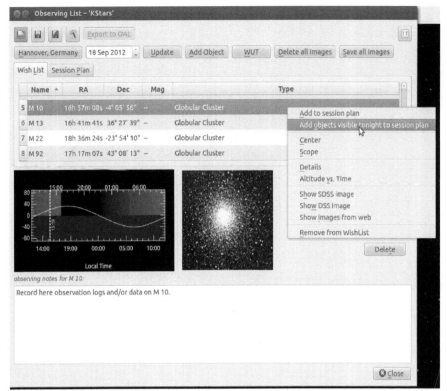

Figure 14: All visible objects from the Wish List are added to the session plan in one single step.

Just mark all objects and then right click on one of them. Choose "Add objects visible tonight to session plan" in order to have all objects in the session plan.

Once done, you can see the visible objects in the session plan, together with a scheduling, when the object is best observed (highest above horizon). Now you know which objects when to look for this night. Good luck!

In the afternoon with Stellarium

The same scenario with Stellarium. By pushing the key "7" we stop the clock. Then we enter time and date in the corresponding window (F5). The date should already be set, but the time must be selected for the setup of the mount.

First, we check the location of Polaris at this time (figure 15). Pressing the "E" key, we turn on the equatorial coordinate grid to see where Polaris is located near the north celestial pole (NCP). Press F3 to find Polaris and center. We get the location of Polaris (figure 15) and as described in the Kstars section, we can use the polar finder scope to align the mount parallel to the earth axis.

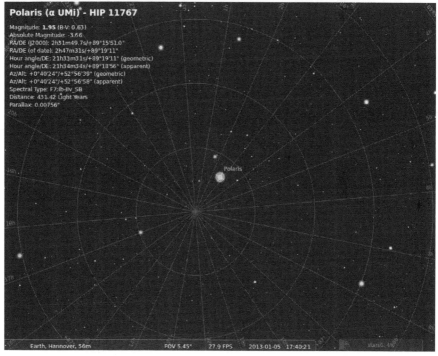

Figure 15: Polaris is located near the NCP. Inversion in the NCP gives the eyepiece view of Polaris in the polar finder scope.

Now we check the visibility of the globular star clusters from table 3. "F3" activates the search window. First let's look for M13.

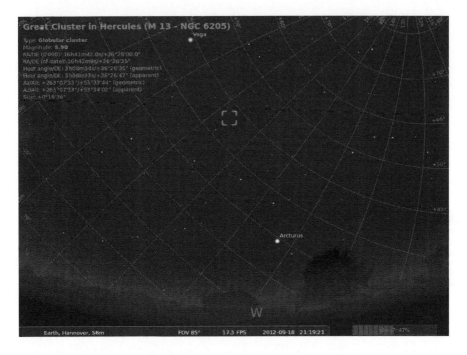

Figure 16: The globular cluster M13 is well visible in the west.

On the 18.9.2012 at 21:19 (MEST), M13 is well visible to see in the west, high enough above horizon (figure 16). Therefore we add it to the list of observable objects. Unfortunately Stellarium does not support an observation list in a sophisticated manner like Kstars: We just have to use paper and pencil, just like with all other objects we want to observe.

The great advantage of Stellarium is the simulation of telescopes, eyepieces and cameras. This allows us to see the object as it will appear on the image sensor of your camera or in the eyepiece of your telescope. With "CTRL-O" you switch the eyepiece view on/off.

In figure 17, you can preview how M13 will be visible through an 40mm eyepiece in an ETX-90 telescope.

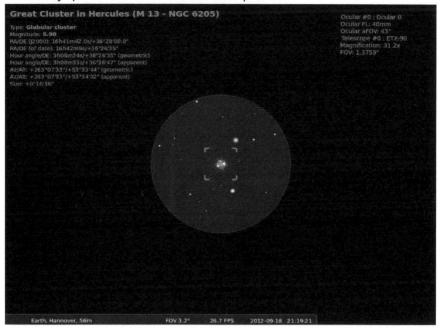

Figure 17: M13 seen in an ETX-90 telescope with an f=40mm eyepiece.

Once you configured your cameras, telescopes and eyepieces within Stellarium, you can preview an exact image of what is seen in the eyepiece and recorded on your image sensor. Figure 18 shows M13 how it would be recorded on the image sensor of an EOS 450D camera. Again, "Ctrl-O" allows to choose from your telescopes, cameras and eyepieces. How to configure your hardware is topic of the next chapter.

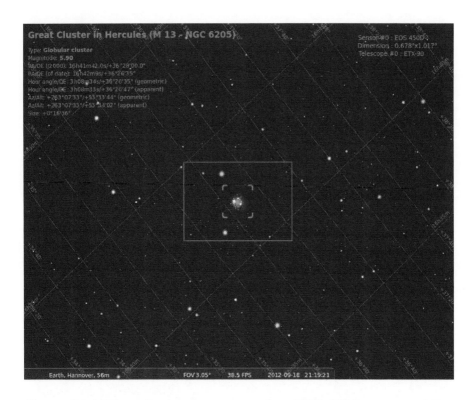

Figure 18: M13 on the image sensor of an EOS 450D camera at the end of an ETX-90 telescope.

Configuring your hardware in Stellarium

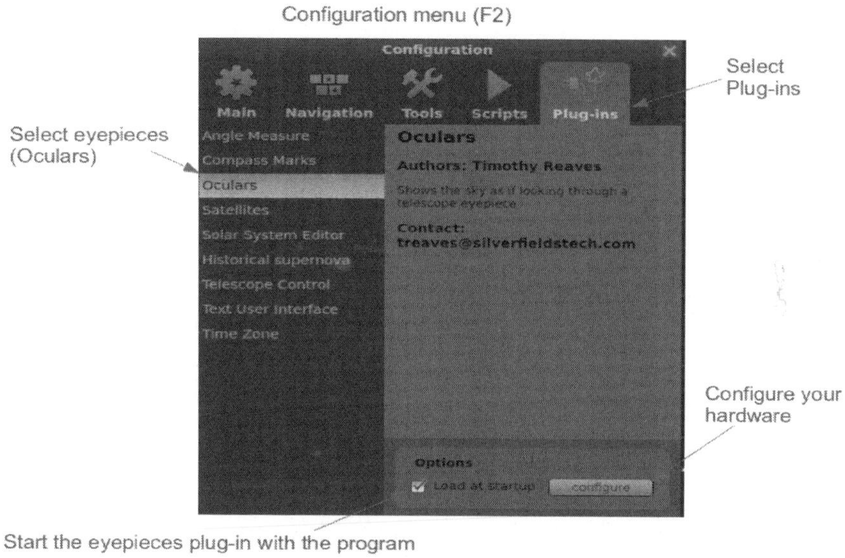

Configuration menu (F2)

Select Plug-ins

Select eyepieces (Oculars)

Configure your hardware

Start the eyepieces plug-in with the program

Figure 19: The configuration of your hardware starts in the configuration menu of Stellarium with "F2".

After pressing "F2", the configuration menu starts. The tab "Plug-Ins" accesses the eyepieces script called "Oculars" (figure 19). A mouse click on "configure" opens the configuration dialogue for telescopes, eyepieces and image sensors (figure 20).

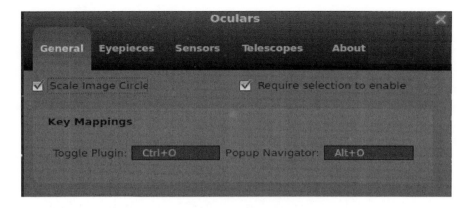

Figure 20: The general part of the Oculars setup remains untouched.

The general part of the Oculars setup remains untouched. A click on the tab „Eyepieces" leads to the setup for eyepieces (figure 21).

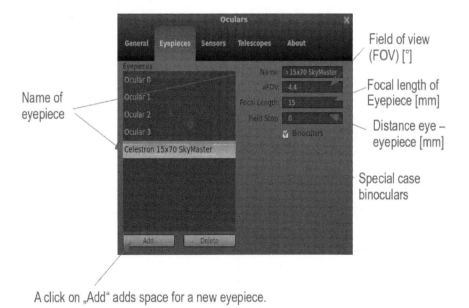

Figure 21: After clicking on "Add", you can enter the data of an eyepiece.

Figure 21 shows the data of the eyepieces already available in Stellarium. You can enter your own eyepieces after clicking on the "Add" button. Then enter the fields on the right side.

The field entry of "aFOV" will limit the field of view on the screen, once you activate the oculars view with CTRL-O. So you can preview the effect of a wide field eyepiece vs. a normal field eyepiece.

Together with the focal length of a telescope, the focal length of the eyepiece determines the total magnification of your telescope (See chapter *Magnification*). Once you select an object, the calculated FOV from the total magnification of the selected telescope and eyepiece is used to show the astronomical object as you would see it in the telescope through the eyepiece.

Next, we add the cameras we are using to take photos. These are entered as "sensors" in the configuration menu (figure 22).

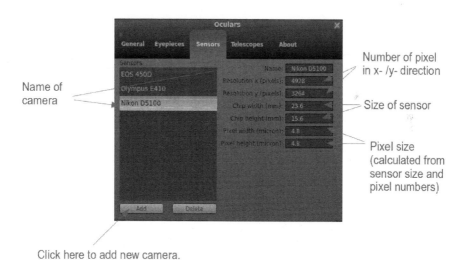

Figure 22: Entering a new camera starts with "Add". The data are stored in the right fields. Except the pixel size, all data are taken from the camera manual.

The camera EOS 450D is already given. Other cameras are added by pressing the "Add" button in figure 22. Again all data are taken from the camera's manual.

Only the pixel size is calculated by the equation:

$$p_{x/y} = \frac{c_{x/y}}{n_{x/y}}$$

Here are:

- $p_{x/y}$ the x- or y-pixel size

- $c_{x/y}$ the size of the sensor in x- or y- direction

- $n_{x/y}$ the corresponding pixel numbers.

Finally the hardware configuration is finished with the telescope data entry (figure 23).

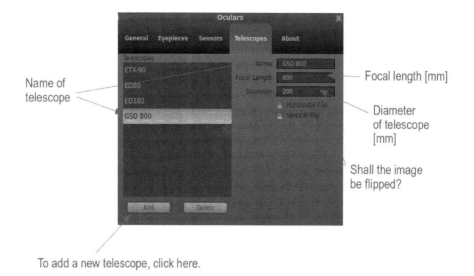

Name of
telescope

Focal length [mm]

Diameter
of telescope
[mm]

Shall the image
be flipped?

To add a new telescope, click here.

Figure 23: After adding a new telescope, the data are input on the right side.

Depending on your demand, you can instruct Stellarium to view the object either completely flipped (as seen through most telescopes) partially flipped (as seen through Newtonian reflectors) or not flipped (as seen by naked eye). Normally a beginner is more confused by these options, so I deselect them.

Once you entered all data, close the window. The configuration is saved and can be activated by the key combination CTRL-O. But before you can do so, you first have to select an object. Figure 24 shows the globular cluster M22 after selection, followed by CTRL-O. Using the ALT-O key combination you can select the eyepiece and / or the telescope. Press again the key combination CTRL-O to switch between ocular view and standard view back and forth.

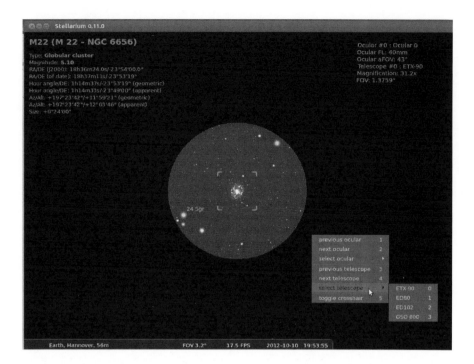

Figure 24: After selecting the globular cluster M22 and activating CTRL-O, you see the ocular view of M22. Pressing ALT-O allows to change telescope and ocular (eyepiece).

If you prefer the camera view of the object, you have to use ALT-O before switching to the ocular view (figure 25).

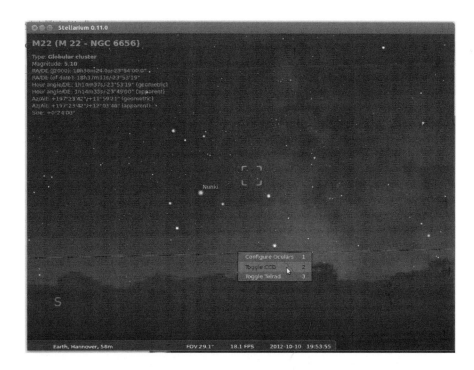

Figure 25: In the normal view you can switch to the camera view with ALT-O.

The first entry in the list of telescopes and cameras will be used. In this case it was the EOS 450D camera and the ETX-90 telescope (figure 26). Pressing again ALT-O allows to change the hardware or toggle back to normal view.

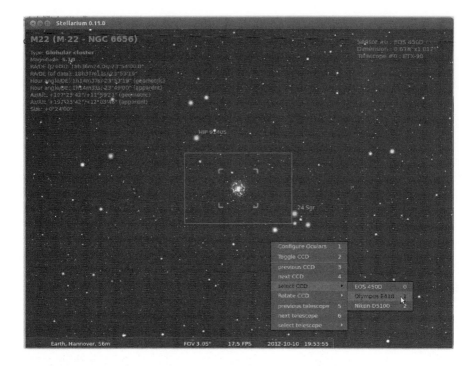

Figure 26: The sensor view was activated using ALT-O. Then ALT-O allows to select the sensor and telescope or toggle back to normal view.

Taking photos

The list of objects is made, the night is dark and the sky is clear. The mount is aligned using the polar finder scope as described using either Kstars or Stellarium. The alignment procedure of the GOTO mount is finished, so the GOTO mount knows where it is looking at and you have a bright reference star in the eyepiece. Now replace the eyepiece with the camera and set the camera into manual mode, select highest sensitivity level and set the shutter to the longest exposure time before bulb mode. This is normally 30s. Switch to live mode if possible or use the optical viewfinder to focus the camera manually on the reference star. Do this carefully and use the strongest magnification in live view possible. Then fix the focus carefully. Make sure the focus cannot move, because you will not be able to control the focus while photographing the astronomical objects on your list.

Now select the first entry from the list of objects and enter its name into the GOTO control. The mount swivels to the first object. Here we go with the pictures. The first photo will probably not be correctly centered. Repeat a photo with a slightly corrected position, using the arrow keys of the GOTO mount. Once centered, do at least 10 photos of the same object, before you swivel onto the next object.

If you photograph near or in a city, the image will have a very bright background, making our object hard to detect. Do not panic, we have the GIMP to improve the image. Nevertheless, the object in the center of the image should be recognized, even if only very weak.

After we photographed an object, we do not immediately swing to the next object but look for a reference star in the vicinity of the object. This one is centered again. Only then do we swing to the object. The reason for this is the usually not so good adjustment when the move is too long. The wanted object generally shows a large displacement. It might even be outside the field of view of the image sensor. And as the object itself is not visible in the live view mode of the camera, a stop at the neighbour reference star helps to correct the displacement. The reference star should be so bright,that it is visible in the live view.

After all objects on the night's wish list have been photographed, we end with a full memory chip and go to bed.

Postprocessing of the images

Now we start with the week of post processing. Yes, it is a time consuming process. And you should do it in several steps in order to not lose precious data. Here comes the textual description. A full color image based description follows later. Experienced GIMP users will prefer this text based description, inexperienced GIMP users might want to step over to the image based description.

Save your images on hard disk

1. **Saving with system.** I use the folder ~/Images/Astronomy for all astro images. Each object gets its own folder in there. In that folder I create a new folder for every observation night. For example, all photos made on 18.9.2012 from M13 go into the folder ~/Images/Astronomy/M13/18.9.2012. As you have taken photos from several objects in a night, you will repeat the procedure of creating folders for every object you made photos of. Then you copy all original untouched photos from the camera chip into the corresponding folders on your hard disk.

Processing the individual images with GIMP

2. **Subtraction of the background.** Every single image is loaded individually into GIMP. Then the color pipette is used to select the color of a background point. A background point might be any point in the image, which is considered to contain no data of stars or the object itself. Clicking on this point with the pipette (color picker tool) sets the foreground color.

3. **Creating a new subtracting plane.** Create a new plane with the selected foreground color. Set the modus of the new plane to "Subtraction". The background of the image should now turn to black. But as normally also parts of the object fall below visibility, set the subtraction from 100% to 90% or less. Let your eyes decide the amount of subtraction.
4. **Saving the processed image as intermediate result.** The original image has a name given by the camera, like DSC_XYZ.jpg, where XYZ are numbers. This name is still shown in the GIMP header line. I now save the processed image as OBJECT_XYZ.jpg, i.e. I replace the camera's name of the image (DSC or whatever) by the object's name. If the image shows M13, I save the image for example as M13_123.jpg, if the original name was DSC_123.jpg. There-fore the relation to the original image is kept.
5. **Repeat steps 2. - 4. for all photos of the same object.** In the end we have the same number of intermediate images as original images in the corresponding folder.

The figures 27-31 show the same steps using the images of the Andromeda nebula M31, taken with my Nikon D5100 at ISO6400 with my ED102 refractor on the HEQ5 mount with 30s exposure time without auto guiding.

Summing up individually processed images

6. **Loading the median number processed image.** There is a time gap of some minutes between the first and the last image taken. Since the mount is never exactly aligned to the earth axis, the object moved a bit in each image. So we load the median number image into GIMP. This image is now our reference image. We switch to 100% view (1:1) in order to work pixel precise in the following steps.

7. **Loading the next image as *"new plane"*.** We now add a new plane with the another image of the object in the same date folder. We now have two layers in the same GIMP image. The newly loaded image is on top of the first loaded background image and therefore covers the background image.

8. **Setting transparency to 50%.** To make both images equally visible, set the transparency to 50%. Now the new image in the foreground is as visible as the old one in the background., allowing us to see the displacement between the two images.

9. **Select the move tool and move the new plane.** Once you select the move tool, you can move the selected plane. It is important to move the newly loaded plane image, not the original image in the background. Make sure that you have set the zoom factor to 100% (1:1) in order to control the movement pixelwise.

10. **Switch off new plane.** This step prepares the repetition of steps 6. - 11.

11. **Change plane mode to *"Addition"*.** The adjusted new plane will be added later on to all other layers. This causes a better exposition of the image, as the light of each plane is added to the other ones. Simultaneously the image gets a noise reduction, as the summation acts like averaging.

12. **Repeating steps 6. - 11. for all images of the same object in the same date folder.** At the end of the process, we have at least 10 precisely aligned image layers, one for each intermediate image. All layers are in the "addition" mode. You should make sure that always only two layers are visible
    a. The background plane.
    b. The plane you are actual working on. All other layers should not be visible. This increases the operation speed.

13. **Save the image in the GIMP format.** There is a lot of work in the image you now created. To save it, make sure you save as a new image in the GIMP format with the ending

*.xcf. Following the proposal of the text before, you would save this image as ~/Images/Astronomy/M13/18.9.2012/M13.xcf. There is no information loss using the xcf-format, which results in a high volume output. 30MB for one stacked GIMP image is nothing extraordinary. The main work is done and we have saved it. What follows is fine tuning, which is still very time consuming.

14. **Switch on all layers.** As we make all layers visible, GIMP is becoming slower and slower with each added plane. Simultaneously you will observe the image getting brighter and brighter with every plane you switch on. Bright stars show up overexposed very soon. That is the reason for the next step.

15. **Tuning the contribution of the layers.** Originally all layers are adding their pixel values to 100% to the pixel in the visible image. Now we reduce the contribution of the individual layers. If we have 10 images in the different layers and set the contribution to 10%, the resulting image has the same brightness as the original images each pixel value is multiplied by 0.1 before it is added to the sum picture, but the noise is reduced. Setting the contribution to a value between 10% and 100% controls the brightening (increase of exposure time) of the image. So we have a tool to control the exposure time after exposition. For astro images normally the rule is: The longer the exposure time, the better. But unfortunately the resulting summary image is still caught in the 8-bit frame of the standard image formats. We need to use compound technologies like HDR or stacking and painting to reduce the burden of 8-bit dynamics in astronomical photos. Thus, we might risk to overexpose bright image parts in order to get the more interesting darker parts of the object better visible later. I will explain that in the chapter Fotoxx, which does just that. Now we try to set the contribution of the layers in such a way, that the resulting summary image shows the wanted structures clearly. We risk some overexposure, which we cure later. In order not to overweigh the

background plane (it is just another plane like all others), we change their status to "Addition" and set the contribution to the same value as the other layers. Then we add a new black background plane in the very background of all other layers.

All in all we control two effects:

- **a.** As we reduce the contribution of layers, the image gets darker, as we increase the contribution of layers, the image gets brighter.
- **b.** We can fine tune the quality by increasing the contribution of good images and decreasing the contribution of images with some problems (e.g. a bit shaken). Let your eye decide.

16. **Save the fine tuned summary image.** You might later on refine the image by starting tuning work from this image. You might prefer a new name for the tuned image like M13_1.xcf for the first variant of your fine tuning work. In any case use GIMP's lossless xcf format.

17. **Save as JPG.** The xcf format is readable only by GIMP, but you may want to upload your images in the web. Therefore it is time to save a copy of your fine tuned image as JPG. This is the version you might also want to print.

18. **Fine tuning of the JPG image.** There are still some unused parameters we can modify to work out details of the object:

- **a.** In all layers of the summary image are still some leftover background illumination. In the summary image these also sum up and may lead to a considerable background illumination. Even worse: The background is normally not equally distributed but has a gradient: More background illumination near horizon, less in zenith. This will become more visible in the summary image and therefore is subject to our postprocessing of the summary image. We now can remove gradients using the same technique as mentioned before, with a slight modification: We create a

new white plane and fill it with the gradient we create
with the pipette tool.

  i.   Select the foreground color FG with the
       pipette at a bright background location.
  ii. Select the background color BG with the
       pipette at a dark background location.
  iii. Select the needed gradient:
       1. Linear gradient for horizon-zenith type
          of gradient.
       2. Circular gradient for gradients caused
          by bad optics.
  iv. Fill the white plane with the gradient tool from
       the FG point to the BG point. You now have
       the gradient plane.
  v.   Subtract the gradient plane from the back-
       ground plane.
  vi. Modify the contribution of the gradient plane
       to your needs.

b. Modification of the gradient curve. With the menu en-
    try "*Color | Curves*" you can change the gradation
    curve. Selecting this tool from the main menu shows
    the histogram of the image, i.e. the distribution of pix-
    els ordered by brightness. You can use the curve for
    luminance (i.e. the total brightness) or separate for
    red green or blue. Lifting up the curve makes the
    pixel below that curve part brighter, pushing down the
    curve makes the corresponding pixels darker. As the
    curve is flexible like an elastic ribbon, you can make
    dark pixels brighter and bright pixels darker.
    Once you have the curve tool active, a right click on
    that part of the image with fine details marks the re-
    gion in the histogram. If you want the details more
    crispy, make the gradation curve around this mark
    steeper rising. Be sure to have the preview button ac-
    tivated, then you can directly control the effect of
    your work.

The extensive description suggests that no more than a single photo can be edited in one afternoon. Probably less.

Next comes the same description as above, but with images.

Image processing with image examples

Select the pipette tool

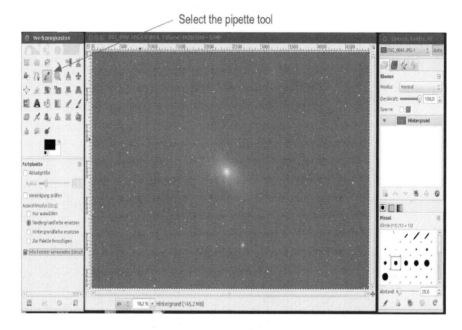

Figure 27: Step 1 - One original image of M31 is loaded. You can see the light pollution in an urban environment. The pipette tool is used to set the foreground color.

Click on background here...

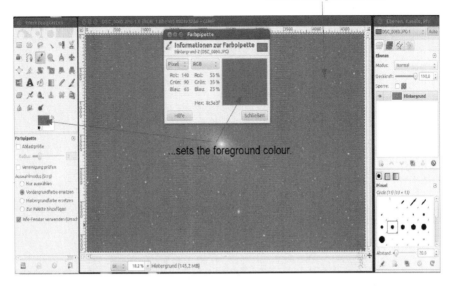

Figure 28: Step 2 - A mouse click with the pipette tool to a background point sets the foreground colour.

Create a new layer with the foreground colour.

Figure 29: Step 3 - Create a new layer with foreground colour.

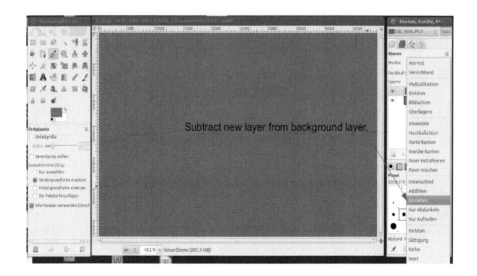

Figure 30: Step 4 - The newly created layer is subtracted from the background layer: Switch the layer mode from "Normal" to "Subtract".

Reduce opacity to 90 (less aggressive).

Figure 31: Step 5 - Reduce the opacity to 90 (%) or less to make the subtraction of the background less aggressive. The background illumination is nearly gone. The image is now saved as M31_XYZ.jpg, where XYZ is the original numbering from the camera.

You have to repeat the above procedure for all images in the same object/date-folder. Once done you have 10 images of the same object with the background illumination (light pollution) removed.

Illustrated description of the summation

Here come steps 6. - 18. with illustrating example images.

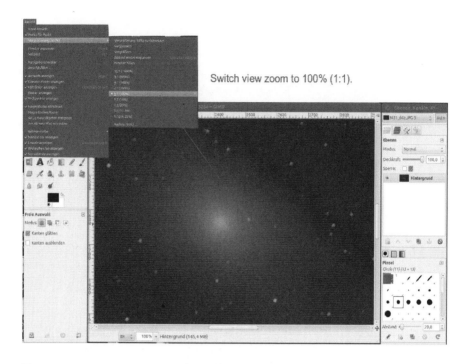

Switch view zoom to 100% (1:1).

Figure 32: Step 6 - Load the median image and switch to 1:1 view (100%). This allows pixel precise working.

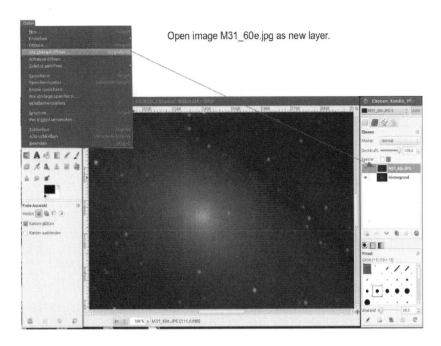

Figure 33: Step 7 - A new image is loaded into a new layer of the same image. It pops up with the name in the layer dialogue.

Reducing the opacity of the upper layer to 50 (%) makes both images visible.

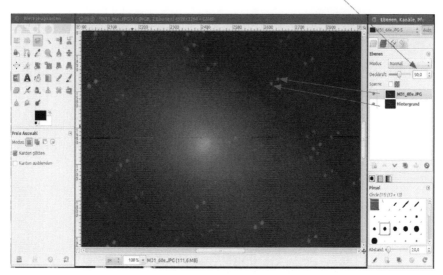

Figure 34: Step 8 - Reducing the opacity of the upper layer to 50 makes both images visible. You can see the drift between both photos.

The move tool moves the active layer and results in aligned layers.

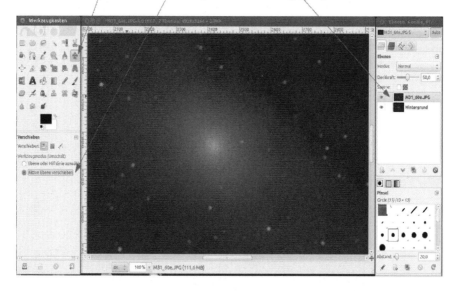

Figure 35: Step 9 - After moving the active layer with the move tool, both layers are aligned pixel by pixel.

All images are added by 22% to the black background (new layer).

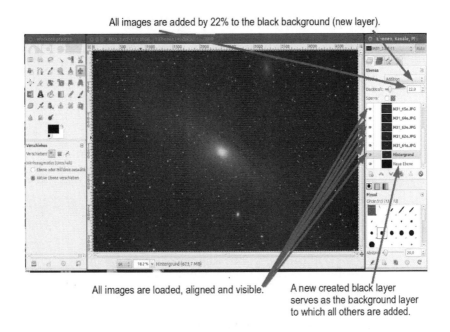

All images are loaded, aligned and visible.

A new created black layer serves as the background layer to which all others are added.

Figure 36: Step 10 - All images are added to the black background layer. The addition is limited to 22% of the pixel value in order to avoid over exposure in the middle part. Note that the image is no longer in the 100% zoom but fills the frame.

This result is saved now as M31.xcf. This file contains all information about layers, layer mode and opacity and is the base file for fine tuning. In addition the same image is also saved as M31.JPG, which is a file usable in all image applications, including web pages. This file is the target for fine tuning as described in the following chapter.

Elaboration of details by changing the gradation curve

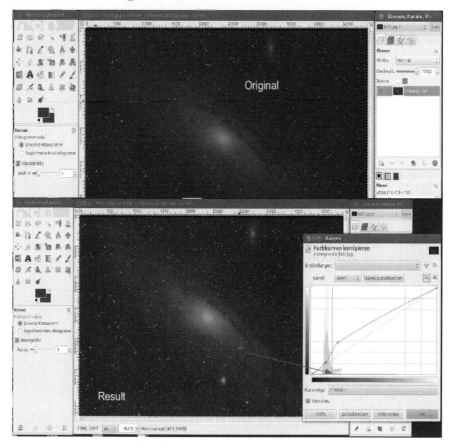

Figure 37: After activating the tool "Colors | Curve" the gradation curve pops up. A click into the nebula (red cross) marks the pixels brightness value (41). Making the gradation curve a bit steeper here causes an improvement in the faint nebula structures.

Removing a background gradient

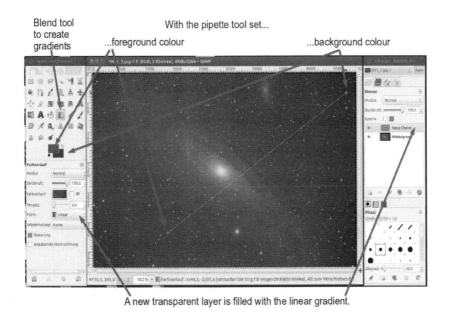

Blend tool to create gradients

With the pipette tool set...

...foreground colour

...background colour

A new transparent layer is filled with the linear gradient.

Figure 38: A linear background gradient is removed. In a first step, the pipette selects the foreground colour, Second the background colour is set. Then a new layer is created and filled with the linear gradient.

The new gradient layer is subtracted by 90% from the background image.

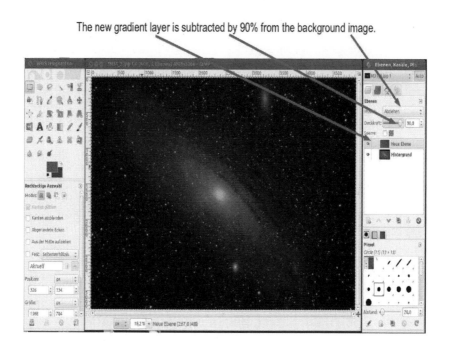

Figure 39: The result of the gradient subtraction is quite impressive. The ugly light pollution is gone.

Post processing of images with Fotoxx

Occasionally astronomical objects show enormous differences in brightness, which an image sensor (CCD or CMOS) cannot handle due to its linear brightness characteristic. As an example, we have a look at an image of the great Orion nebula M42 (figure 40), taken with the GSO 800 mirror and the Nikon D5100 with 400ISO and 30s exposure time.

Figure 40: The sum of 16 images of M42 with 400ISO and 30s exposure time taken by the Nikon D5100 camera in the primary focus of the GS= 800 Newton mirror (f=800mm, d=200mmm). All images are aligned and added by 20% as described in the last chapter.

While the gas tail structures become very well visible by the summation of images, the center of the nebula, the trapezoid, is overexposed.

Each architectural photographer knows about this problem when photographing interior spaces: The window part is hopelessly overexposed, the dark fireplace is disappearing in the shade.

This problem is solved by a digital photo technique called HDR (High Dynamic Range). This technique uses two or more photos of the same object, one with the right exposure for the dark regions, one with the right exposure for the light regions and maybe some more for the midlight regions. Then these photos are mixed together using profile curves. The darker parts finally come from the image with the long exposure, while the light parts are taken from the short exposed image with the light image details. The result is then compiled into one HDR image. Fotoxx is making this procedure quite easy, once you have the photos aligned with GIMP.

Creating an HDR image with Fotoxx

The preparation of the HDR image with Fotoxx is a 4 step process:
1. Start the HDR composite under the menu item "*Combine | High dynamic range*".
2. Selection of images for the composite. A minimum of 2 and a maximum of 9 images can be incorporated into an HDR composite.
3. Modify the profile curves of the images involved.
4. Save the final image.

Preparation (Creation of two images for HDR use)

As the creation of the HDR image requires two different exposed images, we create these before we start Fotoxx and dive into the HDR creation process. We start with the aligned GIMP image of the M42 nebula (figure 40) called M42.xcf and load it in GIMP. As we need two images for the HDR composite, we take the summed up image as one of them. So we save M42.xcf as M42_a.jpg. This is the image, where the dark parts are well exposed, but the trapezoid is over exposed. Next we switch off all layers except one (the base layer) and set this layer to normal mode and 100 opacity. The image is now very dark, the gas tail is nearly invisible, but the trapezoid turns out well exposed. This image is saved as M42_b.jpg (figure 41). Now we have two images, one with good visible gas tail, one with the good visible trapezoid.

Figure 41: A single layer of M42.xcf is visible, all others are switched off. The mode of the layer is set to "normal" and the opacity set to 100. This image is saved as M42_b.jpg.

Step 1

You start Fotoxx and click on the menu item *"Combine | High dynamic range"* in Fotoxx to start the HDR creation process.

Selection of images (Step 2)

After starting the HDR creation (step 1) with *"Combine | High dynamic range"*, the two images, M42_a.jpg and M42_b.jpg, are selected and loaded. Fotoxx tries to find any shifts in the images and to align them. As we did the alignment procedure in GIMP manually, there might remain some shifts, which Fotoxx tries to remove. This is a very cpu-intensive process that requires several minutes on older PCs. During this process, the critical areas of the image will be displayed as red areas. In the bottom of the image appear status information and the keyword BUSY. After completion of the alignment work, a preview of the HDR image is shown.

Modifying the profile curves (Step 3)

How the HDR image is composed from the original images is controlled by the profile curves. After completion of the alignment procedure, the proposed standard profile curves are just linear. The result is in most cases not really bad, but you should keep in mind, that the selection follows a summation rule: The pixel value in the HDR image is calculated from the pixel values in the individual images by multiplying the pixel value in image A with the profile curve A value and added to the corresponding product in image B:

$$p_{HDR}(x) = f_A(x) * p_A(x) + f_B(x) * p_B(x)$$

with:

- $p_{HDR}(x)$: Pixel value at position x in the HDR image.

- $f_A(x)$: Value of profile curve image A at position x.

- $p_A(x)$: Pixel value of image A at position x.

- $f_B(x)$: Value of profile curve image B at position x.

- $p_B(x)$: Pixel value of image B at position x.

In order to get the well exposed tail of M42 in M42_a.jpg not destroyed by M42_b.jpg and vice versa for the information of the trapezoid part of the image, the profile curves should have clear edges. Left of the edge, the dark part is taken from M42_a.jpg, right of the edge, the bright part is taken from M42_b.jpg. Figure 42 shows an HDR preview of the two images, created by two modified profile curves.

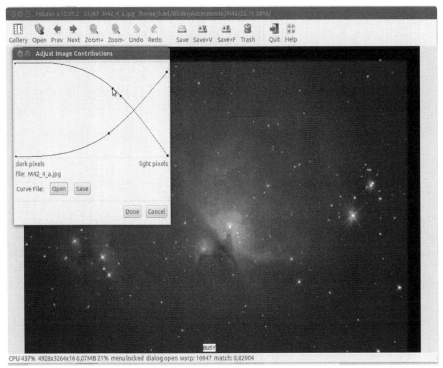

*Figure 42: The HDR composite preview from the images
M42_4_a.jpg (good visibility of the nebula environment) and
M42_4_b.jpg (good visibility of the trapezoid). The profile curves
show clearly the corresponding contributions. Playing with the profile curves can give surprising results. Just try it.*

In this picture, both the trapezoid and the gaseous nebula are easily
recognized. The two profile curves (one for each image) govern the
content of each picture in the HDR preview. The lighter pixels are
primarily from the dark M42_4_b.jpg, the darker pixels come from
the image M42_4_a.jpg.
The modification of the profile curves with the mouse (In the beginning, the profile curves are flat lines) essentially determine the look
of the HDR image. It is a good investment to spend a lot of time on
fine tuning the profile curves.

Saving the HDR image (Step 4)

If you are happy with the composition, the image is saved as a new image. This is done either via the menu "*File | Save to new file*" or by the button "*Save+F*" . In both cases you can determine the location and the image format. Usually you will prefer the * jpg. or *.png format, but also the very memory consuming TIFF format is offered, the latter even with 16Bit/Pixel. If you want to show the images on the web, jpg or png is your choice.

Stack and paint with Fotoxx

There is another technique offered by Fotoxx, which is also useful or even more useful once the range of overexposure is limited to a small area, as in the M42 image above. Again we use the two images M42_a.jpg and M42_b.jpg, created as described in the chapter before. But this time we choose the Stack/Paint technique:

1. Start of procedure by "*Combine | Stack / Paint*".
2. Selection of images for the compound (M42_a.jpg, M42_b.jpg).
3. Painting the final image from the individual images.
4. Saving the resulting compound image.

You can see that the steps are quite similar to those for an HDR compound, except step 1, where a different procedure is selected. Step 3 is the one, which has to be described in more detail, the other ones should be clear from the previous description.

Selection of image for painting (Step 3)

After the alignment procedure, the image is calculated by the average or median of the pixel values in the individual image components. This causes some kind of contrast reduction, which is not the wanted result. Instead we want the dark parts as shown in the bright image and the bright parts as in the dark image (figure 43). Here you can see:

1. The image is calculated by the average of the two contributing images.

2. In the left upper corner you find the control window for painting. You can select any of the contributing images and the size of the painting brush. With this brush you paint the content of the selected contributing image to the location of the brush, once you press the left mouse button. This means, that the calculated average pixel value is replaced by the original pixel value in the selected image under the painting brush.
3. In the compound image, the mouse pointer indicates the actual image range foreseen for painting with the content of the selected contributing image.

In our case, we paint the complete image with M42_4_a.jpg and then the trapezoid with M42_4_b.jpg. The result is shown in figure 44.

Figure 43: The image shows the preview of the Stack / Paint compound image. The contributing images are M42_a.jpg and M_42_b.jpg.

Figure 44: The result of the Stack / Paint procedure shows both well exposed: The faint nebula region from M42_a.jpg and the trapezoid center from M42_b.jpg.

Example images

You will need a high quality print book to see astronomical images in a good quality. But an eBook is not the right place to publish photos. As those who buy eBooks normally have access to the Internet, you will find a selection of my images here [2]. All images are created in the light polluted environment of the city of Hannover, Germany. Just from my backyard. What really surprises is the fact, that under such bad conditions even weak gas nebula like NGC7000 could be photographed.

Technical Addendum

For those interested in the physics of imaging, I try to give a little overview of what is important to keep in mind, when you take your images. There is no guarantee for completeness, but I do my very best to show what is important from my point of view.

Optical paths

Every point of an astronomical object is sending rays of light. Due to the enormous distances in astronomy, we assume the light rays come to us as a parallel beam of rays. To be seen as a point, the beam has to be manipulated by an optical instrument, either a mirror or a lens, to converge into one point. This point of light causes either a signal on the retina of our eye or on the image sensor's surface. We discuss the main optical tools we have for making photos of astronomical objects.

Refractors (telescopes with lenses)

The kernel of an refractor is the image creating lens. In fact it is not a single lens but a compound of several lenses, designed to be free of optical artefacts. In our presentation of telescope optical paths, we simply assume that an ideal lens is working in the refractor.

This is obviously not the case in reality. The most simple lens is an achromatic lens. It is made up from 2 compound lenses [7]. By the combination of the 2 lenses, the chromatic error for the colours red and blue is corrected. Therefore the name of the lens.

With 3 compound lenses, it is possible to create a lens, which is nearly free of chromatic errors [8]. Obviously such a lens is more complex to manufacture and therefore more expensive. To distinguish this type of lens from the more simple achromatic lens, it is called an apochromatic lens.

Unfortunately there are more errors coming up with the creation of images like astigmatism, coma and spherical abberation. The amount of correction is normally directly identifiable in the price of a lens. Again: In my optical paths all lenses are just drawn as a simple lenses, regardless of the type of construction.

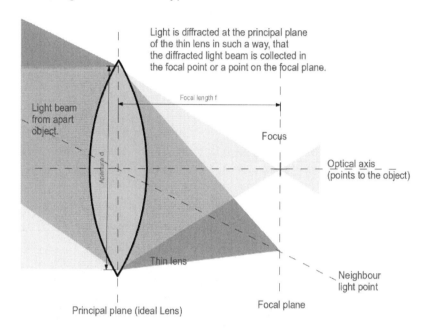

Light is diffracted at the principal plane of the thin lens in such a way, that the diffracted light beam is collected in the focal point or a point on the focal plane.

Focal length f

Light beam from apart object.

Focus

Optical axis (points to the object)

Thin lens

Neighbour light point

Principal plane (ideal Lens)

Focal plane

Figure 45: Light from astronomical objects arrives as parallel light beam. The ideal thin lens (represented by the principal plane) refracts the light into the focal point. Neighboured light points touch down in a point of the focal plane, close to the focus.

In figure 45, you can see the optical path of a refractor lens. If the image sensor of a camera is located in the focal plane of the lens, a sharp image results on the image sensor. The distance from the focal point of the lens to the principal plane of the lens is called the focal length of the lens. It is given in millimeter. Another important number is the aperture d. This is the diameter of the lens in millimeter. The ration $\frac{f}{d}$ is known as aperture ratio, lens aperture or f-stop. This number determines the amount of light getting on to the image sensor. A small f-stop requires less exposure time than a large f-stop, as the amount of light increases with decreasing f-stop.

Have a look at your camera's f-stop settings. You will note the following numbers:

Doubling the amount of light

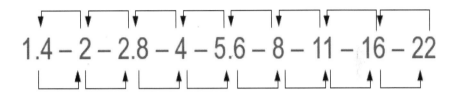

$$1.4 - 2 - 2.8 - 4 - 5.6 - 8 - 11 - 16 - 22$$

Doubling exposure time

For example, a lens with f-stop of 4 will need only half the exposure time of a lens with an f-stop of 5.6, as the amount of light is doubling when the f-stop setting is changed from 5.6 to 4.

Refractor for visual observation

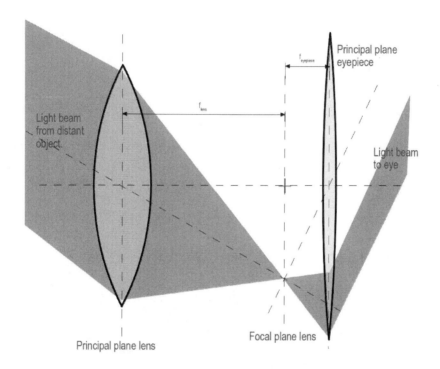

Figure 46: The setup of a Kepler type telescope. The eyepiece works as a magnifying glass, which looks at the focal plane of the lens.

If you want to observe astronomical objects with your eye, the light passing the lens must pass a second lens, the eyepiece. Here the light is refracted again to allow the eye's lens to create a sharp image on the retina. The first man, who described such a telescope consisting of lens and eyepiece was Johannes Kepler. Admittedly, Galileo also described a telescope years before but his construction used a concave lens as eyepiece. Kepler's construction had better optical properties and therefore was accepted as the standard astronomical refractor telescope (figure 46).

In figure 46, however, the eyepiece and the lens are each represented in a wrong relation. The eyepiece has a much smaller diameter than the lens. Here, the artistic freedom has been stressed to correctly display the light beam passing. The eye sees the incident light beam from the eyepiece as a parallel beam of light from a distant object, just under a larger angle. The image appears to be larger. The magnification V results from the focal lengths of the lens and eyepiece:

$$V = \frac{f_{lens}}{f_{eyepiece}}$$

The Newton reflector telescope

The simplest telescope contains a single imaging concave parabolic mirror (figure 47). However, this design has a drawback: If you want to see the image in the focal plane, you obstruct the incoming light. Isaac Newton found a solution for this problem by putting a small secondary mirror in front of the focal plane, that guides the light out of the path of the incoming light through a hole in the tube of the telescope, hence the focal plane is outside the tube (figure 48).

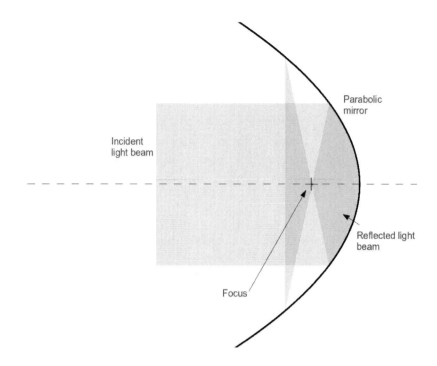

Figure 47: The parallel incident light beam is reflected to the focus of the parabolic mirror.

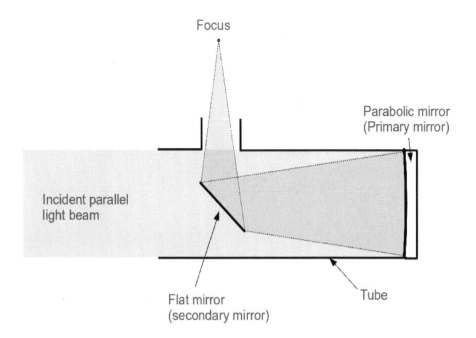

Focus

Parabolic mirror
(Primary mirror)

Incident parallel
light beam

Flat mirror
(secondary mirror)

Tube

Figure 48: The Newton telescope has a parabolic mirror for image creation and a flat mirror for guiding the light beam outside the tele-scopes tube.

Comparing a refractor type telescope with a Newton reflector tele-scope, it obviously has the advantage of no chromatic error. In addi-tion, Newton reflectors can have large apertures [9]. An f-stop of $\frac{f}{d} = 4$ is no problem. Nevertheless focusing such a telescope is a bit critical. A disadvantage is the alignment of the primary and sec-ondary mirrors. This must be controlled frequently.

Other aberrations (mainly coma) are present, but are partly cor-rected by glass elements (lenses). This is recommendable for New-ton reflectors of f-stop $\frac{f}{d} = 4$ for two reasons:

1. The coma is reduced.

2. Digital cameras with changeable lenses suffer from dust. Once dust particles land on the image sensors surface, they will create dark spots in the image until the sensor is cleaned. As the Newton reflector is an open mechanical system, there is a free pathway from the outside dusty world to the clean area in front of the image sensor. The long exposure times that astronomical photos need contribute to the dust particles on the image sensor. A coma corrector closes the open access to the image sensor just like a lens. In fact it is a lens you put into the focuser of the Newton reflector.

The Maksutov-Cassegrain telescope

The Maksutov-Cassegrain telescope also has two mirrors, just like the Newton telescope (figure 49). But the primary mirror has a hole in the middle, and the secondary mirror is a concave spherical mirror carried by a spherical glass plate. The incoming parallel light beam is reflected as in the Newton reflector, then reaches the secondary mirror and is reflected through the hole in the primary mirror out of the telescope tube. There the eyepiece or the camera can pick up the light for further use. The chromatic aberration as well as the coma is not visible, so the telescope creates an image of good quality. A further advantage is the compact and lightweight construction, due to the folded light path. A disadvantage is the reduced

f-stop for these telescopes. F-stops of $\frac{f}{d} = 16$ are usual [10].

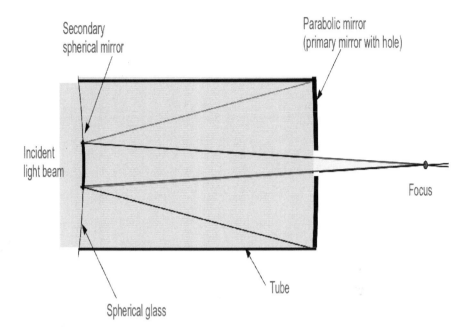

Figure 49: The Maksutov-Cassegrain telescope contains two mirrors and a spherical meniscus lens.

The Schmidt-Cassegrain telescope

This is structured like the Maksutov-Cassegrain telescope. However the front lens is not a simple meniscus-like shape but a quite complex formed glass lens to even better correct aberrations [11].

Magnification

One of the most confusing data once you want to buy a telescope is the magnification. There is a maximal magnification for a telescope and a practical magnification, which is smaller than the maximal possible magnification and responsible for the appearance of an object on the sensor of the camera or in your eye. For each of these applications we will see the formulas.

Visual magnification

Definition

The visual magnification is just the relation of the viewing angle of the object with telescope and without telescope (figure 50).

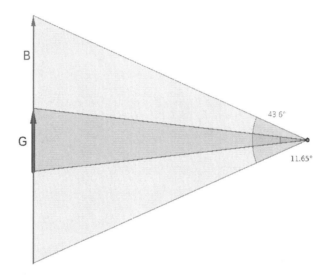

Figure 50: An object G is seen by the angle of 11.6 degrees. Using a telescope, the viewing angle is increased to 43.6 degrees. So the image B seems to be enlarged.

The definition of magnification is:

$$V = \frac{\alpha_B}{\alpha_G}$$

The example in figure 50 then shows a magnification of

$$V = \frac{\alpha_B}{\alpha_G} = \frac{43{,}6\,^{\circ}}{11{,}65\,^{\circ}} = 3{,}74$$

Calculation for a refracting telescope

How do the data of a Kepler type telescope influence the magnification of a telescope?

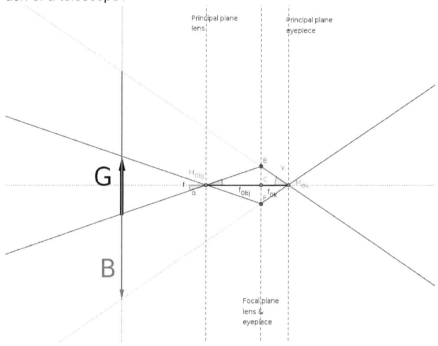

Figure 51: The light beams of the distant object G (Galaxy, star, …) pass through the midpoint of the lens and create an image in the focal plane of the lens, which is also the focal plane of the eyepiece. The eyepiece refracts the light beams as if they originated from the focal plane.

Figure 51 shows how the image B of the object G is formed with the the help of lens and eyepiece. See also figure 46. You can see from figure 51, that the tangent of the lens angle and the tangent of the eyepiece angle are as large as the angles themselves, once the object is far away and therefore the angles are small. Using the definition of magnification this gives:

$$V = \frac{\gamma}{\alpha} \approx \frac{\tan(\gamma)}{\tan(\alpha)} = \frac{\overline{EC}}{\frac{f_{lens}}{\overline{EC}}} = \frac{f_{lens}}{f_{eyepiece}}$$

The visual magnification of the telescope with objective and eyepiece is equal to the ratio of focal length of the lens to the focal length of the eyepiece. The larger the focal length for the same eyepiece, the greater the magnification. Conversely, the smaller the eyepiece focal length with the same focal length of the lens, the greater the magnification. Maximum magnification is thus obtained with a large focal length and a small eyepiece focal length. The wave theory of light is limiting the magnification to a maximum magnification. In practice, this rule of thumb limits the practical magnification:

$$V_{max} = 2 * aperture$$

where the aperture of the lens is measured in millimeters [12] .

Photographic magnification

Unlike the visual magnification, in photography we only have one lens and no eyepiece. So there is no relation of focus lengths. We have to return to the basic definition of magnification: The relation of the viewing angle without lens (naked eye) and the viewing angle with a (telephoto)lens.

In photography, a focal length with the size of the diagonal of the image sensor has been adopted as normal [13]. But in practice, for cameras using the 24mmx36mm format (the original 35mm film format) a focal length of f=50mm has been adopted as normal. For the magnification of a lens, we have to compare the viewing angle of a tele lens with that of a normal lens with f=50mm, when we are talking about 35mm film cameras.

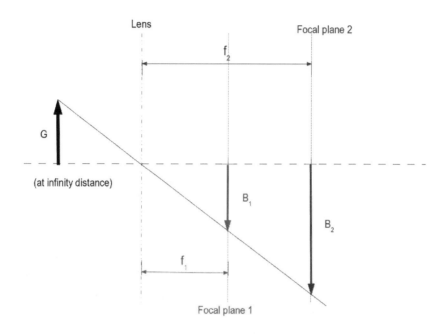

Figure 52: The image of an object at infinite distance is created in the focal plane of a lens. A lens with small focal length (f₁) creates the image closer to the lens. The image B₁ is therefore smaller than that (B₂) of a lens with large focal length f₂. The relation of the size of the two images gives the photographic magnification.

A camera with a tele lens of $f_2 = 100mm$ creates an image, which is larger than the image created with the normal lens of $f_1 = 50mm$. Figure 52 gives a magnification of 2:

$$V = \frac{B_2}{B1} = \frac{f_2}{f_1} = \frac{100mm}{50mm} = 2$$

Size of image sensor and magnification

Once you have an image sensor in the 35mm dimension (24mmx36mm, full format sensor), you can simply adopt the calculation above. The magnification V is:

$$V = \frac{f_{telescope}}{50mm}$$

Unfortunately, with the advent of digital photography, the good old 35mm format has lost its meaning, mainly for two reasons:

1. It is very expensive to manufacture large image sensors. The larger the image sensor, the higher the probability of a defect pixel. That's the reason, why cheap consumer cameras use very small image sensors.
2. The smaller the image sensor, the smaller the normal focal length. A short focal length on the other hand, means a compact camera.

Todays digital cameras most probably have one of the sensors of table 4 built in.

Name	Dimen-sion [mm]	Diagonal length [mm]	Crop factor (magnification vs. 35mm for-mat)	Application
1/ 2.3"	6.2x4.6	7.7	5.6	Compact cameras with-out changeable lens.
2/3"	8.8x6.6	11	4.0	High level compact cam-eras without changeable lens.
FourThirds	17.3x13.0	21.3	2.0	DSLR and mirrorless sys-tem cameras (FT and MFT bayonet).
Foveon	20.7x13.8	24.9	1.7	DSLR with interchange-able lenses. The sensor has a different structure than usual.
APS-C (Canon)	22.2x14.8	27.1	1.6	DSLR with interchange-able lenses.
Full format (35mm)	24x36	43.3	1.0	High valued DSLR or classical 35mm film cam-eras.

Table 4: Dimensions of image sensors in digital cameras ([14], [15], State of 2012).

The diagonal length in table 4 also shows the focal length of the normal lens. As already written, the 35mm normal lens should be f=43.3mm, but for practical reasons has been changed to f=50mm. For the calculation of the crop factor, the real diagonal size has been taken as the column of the diagonal length shows. In order to calculate the magnification, you can bring in the crop factor into the last equation, giving:

$$V = \frac{b * f}{50\text{mm}}$$

Here b is the crop factor from table 4, all other variables are known.

Field of view (FOV)

Looking through a telescope, the field of view is also an interesting quantity.

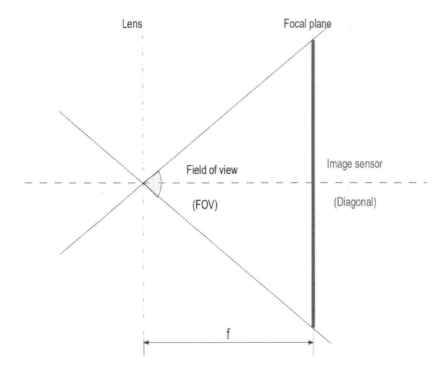

Figure 53: The field of view results from the diagonal length of the image sensor.

According to figure 53, the field of view α is calculated by

$$\alpha = 2 * \arctan\left(\frac{\frac{d}{2}}{\frac{f}{2}}\right) = 2 * \arctan\left(\frac{d}{f}\right)$$

Herein d is the diagonal length of the image sensor from table 4 and f the focal length of the lens (telescope). You do not need to have a crop factor in mind. This is already contained in the diagonal length. You can use this FOV in Kstars and Stellarium to plan the use of the telescope for a certain object. Once you zoom in or out, the FOV is shown either in the low left corner (Kstars) or in the middle of the status line at the bottom window frame (Stellarium).

Telescope f [mm]	FOV [°]		
	APS-C	FourThirds Micro FourThirds	Full size (35mm)
400	7,8	6,1	12,4
714	4,3	3,4	6,9
800	3,9	3,1	6,2
1250	2,5	2,0	4,0

Table 5: FOV for my telescopes and cameras.

Table 5 shows the combinations for my equipment.

Once you have NGC7000 on your target list, Stellarium shows a FOV of 2° for that object. As you need some space around the object, a telescope with a focal length of f=400mm using the FT/MFT or APS-C camera seems useful. A full format (35mm) sensor would need f=800mm or f=714mm instead.

Once you use table 5 to set your FOV in Kstars or Stellarium, you will see the sky as you it appears on your image sensor.

Sources and links

1. http://en.wikipedia.org/wiki/Messier_object
2. https://fotoalbum.gmx.net/ui/external/_W9dkqzRTEC8I02-HsNGVA84801
3. Klaus Gölker: GIMP 2 for Photographers: Image Editing with Open Source Software, ISBN-13: 978-1-93395-203-1
4. http://www.gimp.org/
5. http://edu.kde.org/kstars/
6. http://www.stellarium.org/
7. http://upload.wikimedia.org/wikipedia/commons/thumb/1/15/Lens6b-en.svg/2000px-Lens6b-en.svg.png
8. http://upload.wikimedia.org/wikipedia/commons/thumb/9/91/Apochromat.svg/2000px-Apochromat.svg.png
9. http://en.wikipedia.org/wiki/Newtonian_telescope
10. http://en.wikipedia.org/wiki/Maksutov_telescope
11. http://en.wikipedia.org/wiki/Schmidt%E2%80%93Cassegrain_telescope
12. http://www.nexstarsite.com/_RAC/articles/formulas.htm
13. http://en.wikipedia.org/wiki/Normal_lens
14. http://en.wikipedia.org/wiki/Crop_factor
15. http://en.wikipedia.org/wiki/Image_sensor_format
16. http://www.kornelix.com/fotoxx_de.html

2479607R00060

Printed in Germany
by Amazon Distribution
GmbH, Leipzig